Dilip Bharati was born in the undivided Bengal in 1934. His profound mastery over philosophy, science and advocacy culminates in his literary talent. His first book in Bengali, published in 1975, was an instant critical success and the novels published thereafter acclaimed him as a noted literary figure. Bharati now lives in a small town near the Bay of Bengal with his wife, children and grandchildren.

Muse in Exile

Dilip Bharati

ROMAN *Books*
www.romanbooks.co.in

Poetry Copyright © 2009 Dilip Bharati

ISBN 978-93-80040-01-1

Major Typesetting in Palatino Linotype

First published in 2010

1 3 5 7 9 8 6 4 2

British Library Cataloguing in Publication Data.
A catalogue record for this book is available from the British Library.

ROMAN *Books*
2nd Floor, 38/3, Andul Road,
Howrah 711109, WB, India
www.romanbooks.co.in

Printed and bound in India by
Roman Printers Private Limited
www.romanprinters.com

To my Tutan,

With sublime love
and endearing affection.

Contents

To my Tutan

How long abreast were we
In weal and woe, still
Never did I go well nigh,
Lest browbeaten be.
More feared I, should ye
Be looking at me!

This way gone the days of Spring
Of yours and mine,
This Autumn, the strings of lute
Moaning oft the tunes of pangs
Slowly and softly, I see.

On such a day of grey skies,
Upon the wings of bravado,
Tenderly grapple I and embrace thee.
Paid thou back with a pearly smile
Smeared with a timid kiss
And a euphonic hiss!

Thanks to God and Tutan,
Still the fear, how much of thine oh dear
Comes-o-will to me!

Re-living You

The atrocious time has struck me dead.
But I caress the picture-frame.
'Cos I'm re-living you.
　　The Drop of first rain still lingers—
The sevenseas-gulf was not enough
To keep us apart.
　　Melody and melody kissed my
Unkempt brains!
Hair so dark let me live the
Feverish dream!

A lone table, a dusty phone rings—
Like a gust of wind
The organic trail—your voice it was!
That befell me like the morning rain
And all of a sudden
You and me!
A togetherness!

Do you remember the days of
Those 'debatable topics'
'Are the Indian girls going astray?
Singing the song of wilderness
In bikinis gay?'
No. I mist myself in sandal dew
Of their slender waists!

The mythical maids did so too!
Crystal face in brimful silk!

The wonderlands flooded
Many a kings!
Hapless at the hand of almighty wills!
Modern Venus
Beguiles no more a river than them.

All epics and poems
'Clocking' me of you—
Your eclectic charms!
Blessed is your idyllic pondering wonder!
Shower your beauties
Till the end of this life!
And life beyond it!

The letters—my impromptu thoughts—
Touched your heart.
   As you read my words
Both night and day.
   Yes that's me!
You came to know.
But oh! It was too short a wave!

The unhinged melody came back to me—
The very next day.
The garland of your cosiness
Was the blaze of splendour for me!
You seemed to rise—
And rise still higher
My own fading star!

   I had no hard luck though.
My words were written down on your page.
Recorded the re-recorded . . .
   The copy-right of yours
Is surviving still!

I loved you like death!
And utterly out of breath!

But perhaps God did resent
This immigrant wretch!
A cloud were you!
Destined to will in the nameless Blue!
Just a shadow of glass
Separates us two.

But, till now-not a day left!
Saturated with you
Was the cup of my fate!

Prayer for Salvation

Lift up the deadly curtain,
And show me the ever illuminance!

All's good there—
  happiness only.
Between the two worlds lies
  the stringent impasse,
Wherefrom a caveat uttered:
"Not here, not here, go afar!"

Oh! Ravenous! Should you be back
From the gateway divorced for years?

You have been given thirst . . . hunger . . .
And you have been bestowed the nectary peace
                          and happiness.
May you have the success, the salvation,
May he have nectareous union
  With you,
Through impatient perturbance!

Vivid Waiting

Here the weary days end,
And the swallow-wings bend,
And silent sun quits too quietly.

As I float like sea-weed
A face I see on every street.
A mute trance carries me away.

I sit aghast, to find a shadow,
Even though it gets lost in the meadow,
And the nightmares shake me awake.

When streetlights make love with mists
And flowers are bathed in sugar sweet,
My memory floods me and asks
to wait.

Voice on Air

I waited for the day to end
  To begin again.
At seven a.m.
  I tossed your voice on air.

  The moment you came in my view
Along with those multitudes
  You talked with an aura of glory.

Now that I met you—only the commonest of men—
                    no answer do I need.

After holy births uncountable
My voice on air—I stumble . . .
Today I saw you—my daily voice on air.

The Exit-Bell

My pricking ears
In melancholy fears
Stays awake, in between
All laughter and tears!
The bell may, at any moment, ring.
Well, the inevitable may swing.

Alone!
Haze and fog beckon me within
The stirring of clock's lanky bone!
Could the bell ring?
The bell-man may the ringing bring!

The man attired in black
Reminded me the lack!
And told me not to sleep:
"Wake up man, Your hours now crack!"
O the bell! It nearly rings—
He will fret me with all his whims!

Even the biggest of clamours
Humming of crowd's hammers
Cannot let me be.
There I see the steamers—
My friends! Before the bell rings
                    and before I part,
For you my heart brims—

Unuttered Melody

Sorry be not,
At the outer facet of my address.
Each of us now stand at the verge
                              of our mortality,

The silence now is charming more.
The deep roaring of the waves
                              broken of the sea,
The great panoramic sound of the universe,
And the unheard sound of the formless cosmos—
Remain latent all
In the elemental physique of human beings.

If it be so, then let a few talks with
Tinge of fondness and just a little of timid love
In the seathe of bashfulness,
Rest beneath my breast—

As you jingle your lute of heart
                              at a soft twang,
All the unuttered melodies beneath my breast
Assumes the form.

Still if there be something unuttered . . .
Oh my friend, comprise you may . . .
A hundred times in ever anewed
Semblances in your mind.

Nudity

May the moon spray its lustrous rays
And the Malay breeze tenderly play
Around and through.

Thus you plunge into infinite blue
Like the starry nature—declothed.
May the 'formless' be instilled
Into the riche of the nuance of vellum
Bashfully lured to eye
The manifestation of form.

The unabashed sanctity,
The spotless nudity—
I invite you to the abode of manhood!

Muse in Exile

Long a time ago
Under the shade of oblivion,
You breathed softly,
Upon the soft bosom of life!

Your legs shooting a golden aura
Lightly scented the space between
                     sun and earth.

Your tidy step incites rotundity
And tosses the flowers of poetry.

But . . .

How do we really sing
            the songs of spring now?
Gone are the autumn eves
  And swallow songs
  Tortured are the hymns!

You took your sad sad flight
Beyond the elegiac country churchyard.
Only a wasteland remained—
And dusty muggy nuclear heat.
A grinding machine extricated you
     from the soul of men.

Now that Muse in exile—
Upholds a theatrical glory . . . merely
That speaks no more.

The new-age rules; not love.
Now that Muse . . . is in Exile.

Tagore lent me a sleep
I shall close my weary eye-lids
                              without a word!

No-Cracy

Three thousand years ago, one day I've seen
Dushmanta, the pious king refusing to
Acknowledge his wife and son
In the open session of his royal court.

A still more thousand years back, I saw
The semblance: Rama,
        the Defender of Religion.
To make without hesitance
Innocent Sita
A scapegoat at the feet of the public censure.

Today they are 'Ideal Kings' —
As absolute monarchy
            is absolutely obedient
To the subjects it rules.

Journey

Intelligence

Can't exactly remember where—
In 29th Street or in Tussauds
In that confluence or in that conference—
I saw you first and you me.

Thereafter, on that green carpet
Many a tête-à-tête, many laughter
In the twilight
            of our lives.

That's the beginning . . .
  after the petty loitering to and fro . . .
As others do –
In a sea of places.

One day while sitting in that coffee bar
Said you, "Yes! follow what I said
For times without numbers?
Now we're to come to a decision,
                        aren't we?"
Said I, "Are we in hurry . . . we're
To go a little more afar."
"Parents . . . you know . . .", said you.
"Surely they are to do",
I said, "But for that only exigency you've,
Have ye none?"

"Strange!", your
Reaction, "Long, since long, you've been told.

Oh! I see, you've none to thrash!"

I laughed to see you outraged.

Again you mocked at me, "Heh!
I know your prowess! Ah . . . if ye could be!"
But in the next moment
You started pressing as usual . . .
"Tell out the names, please, please . . .
Yes, you're to say and just now."

I tried to make a fun; said amusingly,
"I can tell you just now but let it be
Hung till tomorrow."

And you started talking to your friend
Who came up by chance
                to save me from the situation.

The Sun sets at the lake.
The evening bell rings out the foggy end.
That 'tomorrow' never turns up.

And the names
Couldn't be known.

A decades passed by this way . . .

And 'that very time' has also ended at
The abyss of the 'Endless Time'.

Knowledge

I remembered the answers of the paramount.
Yudhistir of the *Mahabharata* to one conundrum
Of 'Yama', the god of death, in guise of a heron,
Asked "What's the wonder?" The king
Answered in new dispension: "Man is mortal,
They die everyday. None is to live here for ever.
The livings think themselves immortal still."

Yudhistir in his reply truly put a counter
question: "What can be more surprising
                                        than this?"

Wisdom

In a very calm and quiet
Evening while sitting on the terraced roof
With wife, both afflicted
at the edge of our
Exit from the existence, I suddenly
Glanced at my own foolishness incarnate,
In a trance perhaps standing before
Proclaiming the non-errant new.

"If you two meet,
Would you recognize her?
And would she? Mind the 'time' has
                              leaped forward!
And that very 'time' now is
a silent prayer on the canvas!"

Pondered for a while, I cried out:
"Right you are! Ah, what a fool I'm!"

I remembered
          what the poet said,
"Who says, I won't be there . . . on that morning!"

I was about to put a counter-question
To the incarnate but found him vanquished.

"See, dear, the very question which I couldn't
Dare ask you so far, now do I do.
Don't you inquire him, still today

In the core of your heart, I mean, the brother
                    elderly to your sister-in-law
Hasn't he any nuance of existence
In the niche of the 'core', hasn't he?"

She replied with a loud whisper,
"He's there, why not he be? And what, if
                              he is not there?"

My wife added unequivocally further:
"Nothing harmful in that. So to me,
Harmless are my remembrances of today."

Queer Table-Talk

You are not far wrong!
Both of us could be commodities. Easily!
The sleepers took long enough to awake!
Rend you for rending me,
If you did!

Couldn't agree no more!
See my spears at your feet?
You drove Lear mad:
I knew from then what you could!
The fools wrote 'History'!

Made to play second fiddle?
Destroy the myth or do remember—
There was a Helen; a Cleopatra!
See Eve? Her unequalled power
To take your clothings off?

Timid as we are, we beasts.
Cite those tales where—
You lost without a fight.
A ship, a land, a nation—is of your sex.
We raped them all.

Undaunted, deluded Pearl Harbour,
                    Japan and Clinton saga—
Mere tricks
That weaken not you
But us!
Now, bloom and shoot your wrath!

We have seen some wolves with long dicks!
German et al
Eaten us voraciously
Under the Berlin Wall!
But those were sleepers of us all!

They were seekers of nothing—
Bone-crushing hands!
They were afraid and coward—
They were afraid
Of Virginia Woolf!

Look at the *Mahabharata* and *Ramayana*—
Beware of the new wave—
The Lara Crofts!
And—inform them bastards all!

These cups spoke and left.
The empty chair made the sigh at last!
We are nearing the Absolution.
They are rising—
Awakening tonight!

We are one in love
One in hate
One in pleasure and pain
Sun and Rain
We are no man and woman
But only Human.